Francis Frith's
AROUND EXETER

PHOTOGRAPHIC MEMORIES

Francis Frith's
AROUND EXETER

◆

Dennis Needham

FRITH
BOOK Co

First published in the United Kingdom in 2000 by
Frith Book Company Ltd

British Library Cataloguing in Publication Data

Around Exeter
Dennis Needham
ISBN 1-85937-126-4

Frith Book Company Ltd
Frith's Barn, Teffont,
Salisbury, Wiltshire SP3 5QP
Tel: +44 (0) 1722 716 376
Email: info@frithbook.co.uk
www.frithbook.co.uk

Printed and bound in Great Britain

CONTENTS

◆

FRANCIS FRITH: *Victorian Pioneer*

FRANCIS FRITH, Victorian founder of the world-famous photographic archive, was a complex and multitudinous man. A devout Quaker and a highly successful Victorian businessman, he was both philosophic by nature and pioneering in outlook.

By 1855 Francis Frith had already established a wholesale grocery business in Liverpool, and sold it for the astonishing sum of £200,000, which is the equivalent today of over £15,000,000. Now a multi-millionaire, he was able to indulge his passion for travel. As a child he had pored over travel books written by early explorers, and his fancy and imagination had been stirred by family holidays to the sublime mountain regions of Wales and Scotland. 'What a land of spirit-stirring and enriching scenes and places!' he had written. He was to return to these scenes of grandeur in later years to 'recapture the thousands of vivid and tender memories', but with a different purpose. Now in his thirties, and captivated by the new science of photography, Frith

set out on a series of pioneering journeys to the Nile regions that occupied him from 1856 until 1860.

INTRIGUE AND ADVENTURE

He took with him on his travels a specially-designed wicker carriage that acted as both dark-room and sleeping chamber. These far-flung journeys were packed with intrigue and adventure. In his life story, written when he was sixty-three, Frith tells of being held captive by bandits, and of fighting 'an awful midnight battle to the very point of surrender with a deadly pack of hungry, wild dogs'. Sporting flowing Arab costume, Frith arrived at Akaba by camel seventy years before Lawrence, where he encountered 'desert princes and rival sheikhs, blazing with jewel-hilted swords'.

During these extraordinary adventures he was assiduously exploring the desert regions bordering the Nile and patiently recording the antiquities and peoples with his camera. He was the first photographer to venture beyond the sixth cataract. Africa was still the mysterious 'Dark Continent', and Stanley and Livingstone's historic meeting was a decade into the future. The conditions for picture taking confound belief. He laboured for hours in his wicker dark-room in the sweltering heat of the desert, while the volatile chemicals fizzed dangerously in their trays. Often he was forced to work in remote tombs and caves where conditions were cooler. Back in London he exhibited his photographs and was 'rapturously cheered' by members of the Royal Society. His reputation as a photographer was made overnight. An eminent modern historian has likened their impact on the population of the time to that on our own generation of the first photographs taken on the surface of the moon.

VENTURE OF A LIFE-TIME

Characteristically, Frith quickly spotted the opportunity to create a new business as a specialist publisher of photographs. He lived in an era of immense and sometimes violent change. For the poor in the early part of Victoria's reign work was a drudge and the hours long, and people had precious little free time to enjoy themselves.

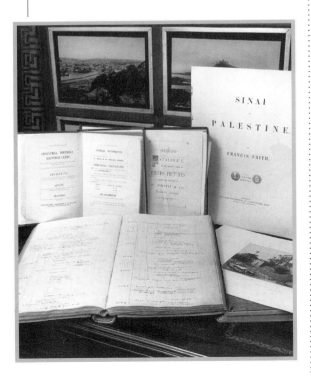

Most had no transport other than a cart or gig at their disposal, and had not travelled far beyond the boundaries of their own town or village. However, by the 1870s, the railways had threaded their way across the country, and Bank Holidays and half-day Saturdays had been made obligatory by Act of Parliament. All of a sudden the ordinary working man and his family were able to enjoy days out and see a little more of the world.

With characteristic business acumen, Francis Frith foresaw that these new tourists would enjoy having souvenirs to commemorate their days out. In 1860 he married Mary Ann Rosling and set out with the intention of photographing every city, town and village in Britain. For the next thirty years he travelled the country by train and by pony and trap, producing fine photographs of seaside resorts and beauty spots that were keenly bought by millions of Victorians. These prints were painstakingly pasted into family albums and pored over during the dark nights of winter, rekindling precious memories of summer excursions.

THE RISE OF FRITH & CO

Frith's studio was soon supplying retail shops all over the country. To meet the demand he gathered about him a small team of photographers, and published the work of independent artist-photographers of the calibre of Roger Fenton and Francis Bedford. In order to gain some understanding of the scale of Frith's business one only has to look at the catalogue issued by Frith & Co in 1886: it runs to some 670

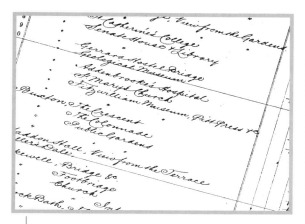

pages, listing not only many thousands of views of the British Isles but also many photographs of most European countries, and China, Japan, the USA and Canada – note the sample page shown above from the hand-written *Frith & Co* ledgers detailing pictures taken. By 1890 Frith had created the greatest specialist photographic publishing company in the world, with over 2,000 outlets – more than the combined number that Boots and WH Smith have today! The picture on the right shows the *Frith & Co* display board at Ingleton in the Yorkshire Dales. Beautifully constructed with mahogany frame and gilt inserts, it could display up to a dozen local scenes.

POSTCARD BONANZA

The ever-popular holiday postcard we know today took many years to develop. In 1870 the Post Office issued the first plain cards, with a pre-printed stamp on one face. In 1894 they allowed other publishers' cards to be sent through the mail with an attached adhesive halfpenny stamp. Demand grew rapidly, and in 1895 a new size of postcard was permitted called the

court card, but there was little room for illustration. In 1899, a year after Frith's death, a new card measuring 5.5 x 3.5 inches became the standard format, but it was not until 1902 that the divided back came into being, with address and message on one face and a full-size illustration on the other. *Frith & Co* were in the vanguard of postcard development, and Frith's sons Eustace and Cyril continued their father's monumental task, expanding the number of views offered to the public and recording more and more places in Britain, as the coasts and countryside were opened up to mass travel.

Francis Frith died in 1898 at his villa in Cannes, his great project still growing. The archive he created continued in business for another seventy years. By 1970 it contained over a third of a million pictures of 7,000 cities, towns and villages. The massive photographic record Frith has left to us stands as a living monument to a special and very remarkable man.

Frith's Archive: *A Unique Legacy*

FRANCIS FRITH'S legacy to us today is of immense significance and value, for the magnificent archive of evocative photographs he created provides a unique record of change in 7,000 cities, towns and villages throughout Britain over a century and more. Frith and his fellow studio photographers revisited locations many times down the years to update their views, compiling for us an enthralling and colourful pageant of British life and character.

We tend to think of Frith's sepia views of Britain as nostalgic, for most of us use them to conjure up memories of places in our own lives with which we have family associations. It often makes us forget that to Francis Frith they were records of daily life as it was actually being lived in the cities, towns and villages of his day. The Victorian age was one of great and often bewildering change for ordinary people, and though the pictures evoke an impression of slower times, life was as busy and hectic as it is today.

We are fortunate that Frith was a photographer of the people, dedicated to recording the minutiae of everyday life. For it is this sheer wealth of visual data, the painstaking chronicle of changes in dress, transport, street layouts, buildings, housing, engineering and landscape that captivates us so much today. His remarkable images offer us a powerful link with the past and with the lives of our ancestors.

TODAY'S TECHNOLOGY

Computers have now made it possible for Frith's many thousands of images to be accessed almost instantly. In the Frith archive today, each photograph is carefully 'digitised' then stored on a CD Rom. Frith archivists can locate a single photograph amongst thousands within seconds. Views can be catalogued and sorted under a variety of categories of place and content to the immediate benefit of researchers. Inexpensive reference prints can be created for them at the touch of a mouse button, and a wide range of books and other printed materials assembled and published for a wider, more general readership - in the next twelve months over a hundred Frith local history titles will be published! The

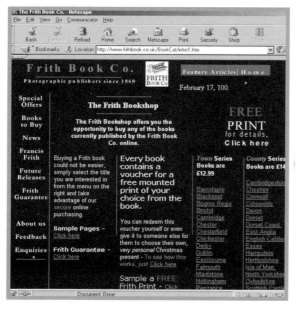

See Frith at www. frithbook.co.uk

day-to-day workings of the archive are very different from how they were in Francis Frith's time: imagine the herculean task of sorting through eleven tons of glass negatives as Frith had to do to locate a particular sequence of pictures! Yet the archive still prides itself on maintaining the same high standards of excellence laid down by Francis Frith, including the painstaking cataloguing and indexing of every view.

It is curious to reflect on how the internet now allows researchers in America and elsewhere greater instant access to the archive than Frith himself ever enjoyed. Many thousands of individual views can be called up on screen within seconds on one of the Frith internet sites, enabling people living continents away to revisit the streets of their ancestral home town, or view places in Britain where they have enjoyed holidays. Many overseas researchers welcome the chance to view special theme selections, such as transport, sports, costume and ancient monuments.

We are certain that Francis Frith would have heartily approved of these modern developments, for he himself was always working at the very limits of Victorian photographic technology.

THE VALUE OF THE ARCHIVE TODAY

Because of the benefits brought by the computer, Frith's images are increasingly studied by social historians, by researchers into genealogy and ancestory, by architects, town planners, and by teachers and schoolchildren involved in local history projects. In addition, the archive offers every one of us a unique opportunity to examine the places where we and our families have lived and worked down the years. Immensely successful in Frith's own era, the archive is now, a century and more on, entering a new phase of popularity.

THE PAST IN TUNE WITH THE FUTURE

Historians consider the Francis Frith Collection to be of prime national importance. It is the only archive of its kind remaining in private ownership and has been valued at a million pounds. However, this figure is now rapidly increasing as digital technology enables more and more people around the world to enjoy its benefits.

Francis Frith's archive is now housed in an historic timber barn in the beautiful village of Teffont in Wiltshire. Its founder would not recognize the archive office as it is today. In place of the many thousands of dusty boxes containing glass plate negatives and an all-pervading odour of photographic chemicals, there are now ranks of computer screens. He would be amazed to watch his images travelling round the world at unimaginable speeds through network and internet lines.

The archive's future is both bright and exciting. Francis Frith, with his unshakeable belief in making photographs available to the greatest number of people, would undoubtedly approve of what is being done today with his lifetime's work. His photographs, depicting our shared past, are now bringing pleasure and enlightenment to millions around the world a century and more after his death.

AROUND EXETER – *An Introduction*

YOU CAN ARRIVE in Devon by plane, train or car. Travelling along the A30 trunk road, you will be following a course similar to that chosen by the Romans two thousand years earlier. You can come along the A38 from the midlands, or use the modern M5 which actually by-passes the city. Motorways are undoubtedly fast and convenient for the long-distance traveller; but what they do not do is allow you to discover this lesser-known treasure of England, the ancient city of Exeter.

The Romans established their most westerly fortress here in 55AD when Isca Dumnoniorum was chosen as a base for the 2nd Augustan Legion. The formidable barrier of Dartmoor must have been something of a deterrent to detailed exploration beyond, although there are many examples of Roman development further west. Later, a walled town was built here, and there are many remains of those Roman days still to be seen within the city. Even the main thoroughfare - High Street - is believed to be based on the old Roman road.

After the legions were forced to leave Britain, there is a hiatus in our knowledge of the Exeter area lasting nearly two hundred years. Then, in the 7th century there are records of a monastery; by the 9th century, Alfred the Great was fighting the Danes out of Devon, and is believed to have spent time here.

As is the case in so many of our great cities, it was the establishment of religious settlements that became the catalyst for real development. Before the Normans arrived, Exeter had become a see with its own bishop. For well over a century, the see in this corner of Devon had been in Crediton. It was bishop Leofric in 1050 who obtained papal permission to move his see behind the walls of Exeter. The magnificent cathedral was built a century later, and subsequently various priories and friaries were established.

Exeter had a mayor by 1205; it was second only to Winchester in provincial cities, and the establishment of a port had much to do with the wealth created hereabouts. But a combination of a silting river and a weir constructed by a local noblewoman saw trade move downriver towards Topsham. It was not until the opening of the canal in 1566 that it was possible to trade directly into the city again. Because of its proximity to good sheep country, wool has always played a major part in the economy of Exeter. The Worshipful Company of Weavers, Fullers and Shearmen of the City of Exeter ruled the roost for many a long year; Tuckers Hall still exists on Fore Street.

But this part of Devon has also displayed something of a stubborn streak over the centuries. The city resisted the advances of William the Conqueror in 1068 and was under siege for eighteen days before it fell. Rougemont Castle, on the highest point in town, was constructed as a result of that fracas. The city was attacked again in 1497 when the Flemish pretender to the throne, Perkin Warbeck, tried to enter with his small army. He failed at that time, but soon succeeded in making an entry - in chains. Henry VII held him here before removing him to the Tower of London and a date with the executioner.

After the Dissolution of the Monasteries, a large portion of the populace rejected the new religion, wanting to stay with Rome. This occasioned more bloodletting. But it was nothing to the gore that flowed after the Monmouth uprising. It was during the reign of James II that the Duke of Monmouth rebelled and was defeated at the Battle of Sedgemoor in Somerset. Some of the rebels were brought to Exeter, where the infamous Judge Jeffries held one of his Bloody Assizes: 80 rebels were hanged here.

Peace and prosperity then reigned until a frightening event took place in the spring of 1942. On the explicit instructions of Adolf Hitler, several of England's more attractive cities were targeted for what he called 'reprisals'. He claimed that the British bombing of the port of Lubeck had caused many casualties, and that therefore the German's terrorising of the civilian population was justified. On three successive nights at the end of April and again in May, bombs rained down on the city. 1700 buildings, including some of the finest Regency houses in the city, were destroyed in these raids. A further 14,000 were damaged, and civilian casualties were heavy. The cathedral suffered from the effects

of a 500lb bomb which demolished three bays of the south choir aisle. Luckily, much of the precious ancient glass and portable objects had previously been moved to a place of safety; the cathedral would be rebuilt and the valuables eventually returned.

With the coming of peace, rebuilding the centre of Exeter became a priority. It is sad country. It brought a degree of wealth and prosperity to the city, and created its own little world around the canal basin. Much of this can still be seen today. The Customs House was the first brick house in Exeter, and is now preserved. Several of the surrounding buildings create an authentic atmosphere much admired by both film and television produc-

that lack of flair and unsuitable building materials have created several areas of utter boredom. Gone are the flowing Regency lines, which are replaced by bland red brick and dirt-streaked concrete. But overall the city is still a place of compelling attraction. Because the old centre is so compact, a walking tour of the whole place is easy to undertake. The arrangement of photographs in Chapter Two is roughly the route of a walk around the town, after a look at the cathedral and its surrounding area.

Beyond the town centre, the river is a focus of attention, followed by the canal. This was the first artificial navigation with locks in this ers looking for locations for their period pieces. One of the most famous - the television series 'The Onedin Line' - was filmed here. It is sad to report that activity on the canal is now minimal. The Museum has dispersed, and the only commercial trade - a ship carrying sewage slurry out to sea for dumping - ended at the end of the last century.

The other major transport revolution was, of course, the arrival of the railways. This part of the country was the domain of that greatest of early railway engineers, Isambard Kingdom Brunel. The Bristol and Exeter Railway opened in the spring of 1844, and the continuation towards Torquay and Plymouth was opened in 1849. Exeter would become a rail cross-roads with branch lines to both north and south; with the arrival of the London and South Western Railway in 1860, expansion would continue as this company moved into northern Devon and Cornwall. In later years, these lines would become known as 'the withered arm' of the Southern Railway.

Fortunately for us, Francis Frith and his pioneering band of photographers did not confine their activities to the city alone. Realising that there were some simply wonderful villages in the surrounding countryside, they travelled the byways of Devon searching out those special scenes which make this collection unique.

Topographically, the area is dominated by the valley of the river Exe. Indeed, it was at the lowest crossing point of the river that the Romans built their fortress. It is surprising to discover that the Exe rises way up in the north of Devon, only a few miles from the Bristol Channel. The Yeo and Culm join the Exe just north of Exeter, and most of our featured villages will be found alongside these waters. Despite their similarities, the villages are as diverse as England itself. Pure tradition will be found in the cob-and-thatch villages of Newton St Cyres, Dunsford and Rockbeare. These are a contrast to Topsham, which has the air of a decaying estuary port about it - and yet is full of life.

It is generally assumed that Topsham was the first place that the Romans landed in Devon. Certainly there is an ancient record of the place, and another mention of the town at the time of Domesday, when an active salmon fishery was recorded. Walk down The Strand, which runs parallel with the river, and admire the early 18th-century Dutch-style houses, built by prosperous local merchants. The remarkable Salutation Inn on Fore Street dates from 1720, and there are several other venerable pubs. Most of the roads which run off the Strand are worthy of exploration, as is the High Street. The 20th-century craze for modernisation and redevelopment seems to have left Topsham relatively unscathed. This owes much to the fact that there are only two roads into the town, making it something of a dead end. Thus, the onward march of the motor car has stalled to some degree here - but not completely: for to the north, the soaring viaduct which carries the M5 motorway 690 yards over the Exe valley interposes itself between Topsham and its view towards Exeter.

One of the great pleasures of exploring both town and village is to carry this volume along with you. Enjoy the experience of working out just where our photographer set up his equipment all those years ago. As you snap away at the same view with your automatic camera, picture the back-breaking load of equipment those pioneers carried.

Marvel at how little our green and pleasant land has changed during the intervening years. Or perhaps you will frown at the wanton destruction of the eye-pleasing views - recorded by the Frith cameramen - by the architectural nightmares that sometimes stand in their place. Wonder at the acres of green fields that have disappeared under a welter of bricks and concrete.

This is a book for all seasons. Muse over it from your armchair during the long winter months. Then travel around during the more pleasant summer days. But, above all, enjoy the sheer pleasure of nostalgia as displayed within these covers.

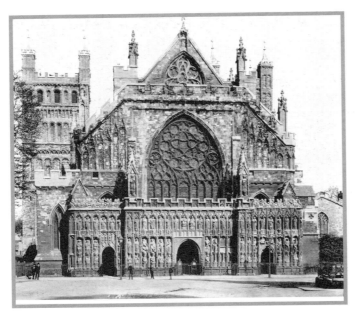

THE CATHEDRAL, WEST FRONT 1887 19601

THE CATHEDRAL
West Front 1887

If this looks magnificent, then looks do not deceive. This gorgeous west front of Exeter Cathedral is but a taster for what lies behind the door. The work here dates from 1329-42, although there are some Norman parts to be found. A statue of St Peter, the patron saint, is located high on the gable.

◆

THE CATHEDRAL
West Front c1955

This study illustrates the essentially timeless nature of our great ecclesiastical buildings. The only changes are a few cars and different fashions; there is not even any evidence of the depredations wreaked upon the building by the Luftwaffe.

THE CATHEDRAL, WEST FRONT c1955 E48011

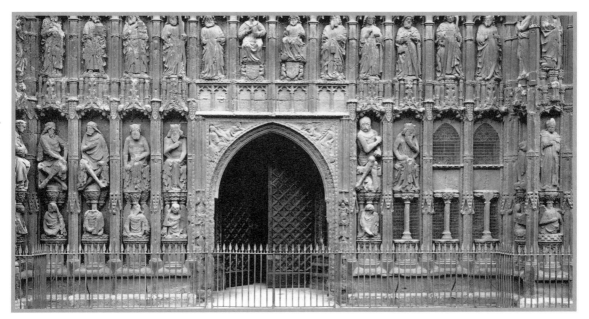

THE CATHEDRAL, WEST FRONT 1924 76587A

A detailed study of the carvings reveals English kings, priests and soldiers. Note the kings sitting cross-legged. You can see similar poses in the cathedrals of Lichfield and Lincoln. Angels, prophets and apostles are also depicted by those long-dead craftsmen.

THE CATHEDRAL, NAVE EAST 1896 37998

The soaring grandeur of the vaulting, the great choir screen and the organ case are the main features of this magnificent view of the nave. The sheer scale of the work and the skill shown by craftsmen almost 700 years ago is still awe-inspiring.

THE CATHEDRAL, CHOIR EAST 1924 75974
You soon run out of superlatives when looking at something so majestic. The choir stalls are Victorian, but the window glass is 14th-century. This was saved from destruction during the bombing by being removed and stored in a safe place. Note the Bishop's Throne to the right, which was made in 1316. It is 59ft high, and is made completely of wood: everything is held together by wooden pegs. Today, the altar has changed significantly.

THE CATHEDRAL 1924 76579
At this stage in its life, the stonework is starting to look a little worn and grubby. It was in 1970 that the cleaning and restoration work started. The finished product is most pleasing to the eye. The roof, incidentally, is the longest ever built in the Pointed style of architecture.

THE CATHEDRAL, SOUTH-EAST VIEW 1887 19603

THE CATHEDRAL
South-East View 1887

This view of the south-east corner was taken long before aerial warfare was known. This was the corner that suffered the most damage in the air raids of 1942. Reconstruction and repairs were soon in hand, and today it is impossible to see the join.

THE CATHEDRAL c1955

This is a view now no longer to be seen. Extensive building has taken place in this area, replacing the buildings flattened in the war. An 'O' model Bedford tipper truck is in the foreground. These lorries were the workhorses of the immediate post-war period. Here, they would have been employed removing demolition rubbish to the tip and returning with whatever building materials were available at the time.

THE CATHEDRAL c1955 E48028

MOL'S COFFEE HOUSE 1906 53783

MOL'S COFFEE HOUSE 1924 76591

MOL'S COFFEE HOUSE 1906
Cathedral Yard - the road on the left - is still a grand affair with a range of businesses. Street lighting at this date is still by gas, and there is not a hint of a mechanised vehicle.

MOL'S COFFEE HOUSE 1924
This building has so much history it would need a book of its own. What you see from the outside is essentially 17th-century, with the Dutch-style gable added around 1885. What is hidden is the interior. Much of this is 16th-century, and it is known that Raleigh, Hawkins, Drake and other seafarers who gave us so much, frequented this very building.

MOL'S COFFEE HOUSE c1955

This is an identical view to photograph No 76591, but taken over a quarter of a century later. The whole place has been spruced up and looks cared for. Worth & Co, picture framers, cleaners and gilders, are no more. Today, Eland's sell maps, atlases and globes from the premises.

◆

THE ROYAL CLARENCE HOTEL & MOL'S COFFEE HOUSE c1960

Compare this scene with photograph No 53783, taken from almost the same spot. Cars are everywhere, and the Exeter Bank (founded 1769) has been taken over by the Royal Clarence Hotel, which now has a fine canopy over its main entrance. The church (St Martins) is an old one, consecrated on 6 July 1065. It is no longer in use; the Churches Conservation Trust now take care of it. The iron railings disappeared for munitions production during the war.

MOL'S COFFEE HOUSE c1955   E48069

THE ROYAL CLARENCE HOTEL & MOL'S COFFEE HOUSE c1960   E48037

THE DEVON AND EXETER HOSPITAL c1955 E48063

THE DEVON AND EXETER HOSPITAL c1955

The Royal Devon and Exeter hospital still provides care for inhabitants of this city: but not on this site in Southernhay. The area health authority have used these delightful Georgian buildings as offices since 1974. Health care has moved to other sites further from the town centre.

◆

ROUGEMONT CASTLE 1924

Rougemont Castle was one of the earliest Norman fortifications, established in 1068 after William captured the town following a rebellion. It is said that Caesar built a fortification on the same spot a thousand years earlier. Most of the area is now ruins. This gate, the entrance to the inner bailey, was built around 1770, and the portcullis is for show only.

ROUGEMONT CASTLE 1924 75980

ROUGEMONT CASTLE 1924
The lady and her children, heads well shaded against the summer sun, are taking their ease on one of the many seats provided hereabouts. You can see similar scenes to this day.

ROUGEMONT CASTLE 1924
A tower and some of the wall can be identified in this view, taken in Northernhay Gardens. Today, Exeter still takes its ease here. Note the old perambulator, well laden with youngsters. The low wall in the foreground is the site of the war memorial which will be looked at in detail in photograph No 75993.

ROUGEMONT CASTLE 1924 75981

ROUGEMONT CASTLE 1924 75982

ROUGEMONT CASTLE GARDENS 1924 75984

The castle is off to the left in this view of the gardens. There are few people moving around; just the lady who seems to be studying the gorgeous floral displays. As before, the seats are occupied - one by a couple of gentlemen appropriately hatted.

THE WAR MEMORIAL 1924 75993

This Memorial was erected soon after the 1914-18 war as a tribute to those who died. On the face immediately below the soldier in his greatcoat, a new plaque has now been added. It simply adds the names of the fallen in the 1939-45 war. With the horrors of the first war fresh in their memory, the people close by are clearly showing a degree of respect.

THE WAR MEMORIAL 1924

Our photographer has moved to the right - roughly where the lady and gentleman are standing in the photograph No 75993 - to take this picture. The inscription on the plinth is now clearer. It reads: 'In proud and grateful memory of the men and women of Exeter and Devon who gave their lives in the Great War 1914/18. Their name liveth for ever'.

NORTHERNHAY 1900

An early view of Northernhay, almost devoid of people. Note the lamp standards, clearly providing electric lighting: given the date of the view, this is a very early use of electricity.

THE WAR MEMORIAL 1924 76595

NORTHERNHAY 1900 46041

THE ROUGEMONT HOTEL 1924 76603

The Rougemont now has the suffix 'Thistle' to its name, denoting its membership of a chain. The wall (left) and gateposts have been reduced to half their height here, the creeper is off the wall and the chimney stacks on the right-hand section have gone. Otherwise, there is little change today. Note the standard carrying the tram wire. The service from both train stations ran along here.

BULLER STATUE 1931 84066

THE CLOCK TOWER 1929 82298

BULLER STATUE 1931
The statue is in memory of a local hero. Sir Redvers Henry Buller was born in Crediton in 1839 and served with the 60th Rifles. He was Commander-in-Chief in the 2nd Boer War (1899-1900) and raised the Siege of Ladysmith in 1900. He died in 1908. The bronze statue was erected in 1905.

◆

THE CLOCK TOWER 1929
Located at the junction of New North Road and Queens Street, only a few yards away from Sir Redvers Buller, this Gothic creation was constructed as part of the Diamond Jubilee celebrations of Queen Victoria in 1897 and was designed by T H Andrews. Hemlines visible to the right are considerably higher than those in the earlier photographs in this book.

HIGH STREET AND THE POST OFFICE 1896 38011
The High Street is totally different today. There are familiar names here though: the Boot Stores on the left carries the name Stead & Simpson on the fascia. The grand building on the right is the post office, and further up the street there appears to be a huge ladder against the Cathedral Dairy Company building.

HIGH STREET 1896 38012
This view was taken the same day as photograph No 46044, but looking the other way: the edge of the post office is to the left. Gas lighting is still in use, and the traders' awnings provide poles for tethering horses or for leaning those new-fangled bicycles against. All this scene is now gone for ever.

HIGH STREET 1900 46044

It is just four years after photograph No 38011, and a little further down the street remarkable changes are taking place. Bicycles are the 'in' thing: there are five of them in this view alone. They still have unsurfaced roads to contend with. The shop (extreme left) is the Victoria Bazaar Coy, No Article Over 6 1/2d (3p today).

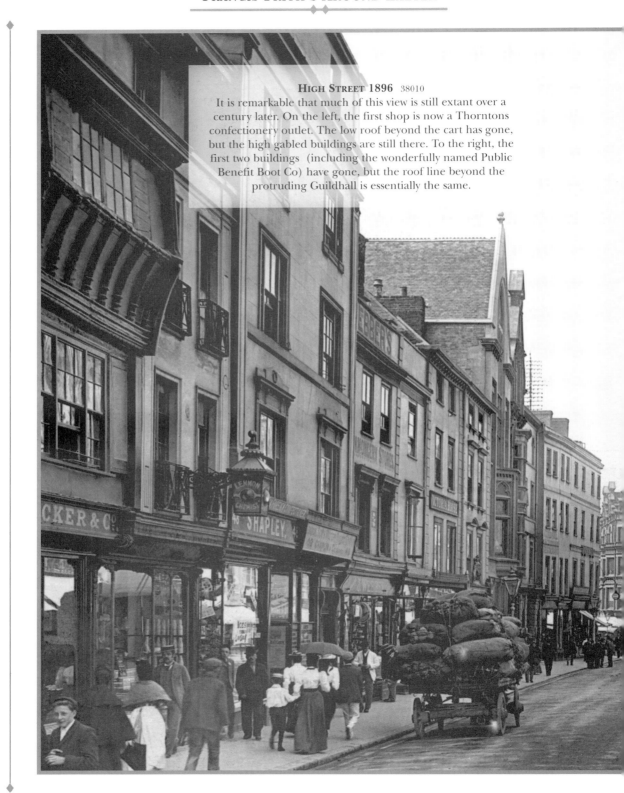

HIGH STREET 1896 38010

It is remarkable that much of this view is still extant over a century later. On the left, the first shop is now a Thorntons confectionery outlet. The low roof beyond the cart has gone, but the high gabled buildings are still there. To the right, the first two buildings (including the wonderfully named Public Benefit Boot Co) have gone, but the roof line beyond the protruding Guildhall is essentially the same.

HIGH STREET 1896 38013A
This view evokes memories of an age for ever past. Here we see horse-powered transport and a shop trading as 'Hatter and Hosier'. This whole scene no longer exists.

HIGH STREET 1896 38014
At the corner of Queens Street, the
main building on the left has now gone,
but the two venerable ones beyond are
still there. Note that the shop sells
'albums, cases and fancy goods', and
according to the banner in the window it
is the 'Last week of Sale'. Could it have
been
a closing down sale? Because the
next view . . .

HIGH STREET 1900 46043
...taken just four years later shows a change of proprietor. The London & South Western Railway cart is making a delivery to the shop. Note also that street lighting is now electric. Also, admire the ornate pole: our Victorian forefathers certainly had style. The building is now replaced by a rather ugly construction built in 1971 and housing the retailers C & A.

OLD HOUSES 1924 76592
These houses are in the High Street. The left-hand building is no more; mercifully the half timbered one still endures. The frontage is all that has altered and the current tenants - Lakeland - are no longer selling Pig Pen equipment as advertised in the window. The right-hand building advertises itself as Hosiers, Tailors, Outfitters, Glovers. The inscription still exists, even if the use of the building has changed.

ST STEPHEN'S CHURCH 1924

This pretty little church is on the High Street. It is a wonderful mix of periods: Norman columns with a neo-gothic interior. The outer walls date from 1664, when much of the building was destroyed by fire. The benefactor who provided funds for this work was George Potter, and he is remembered by a wall monument inside the church.

◆

HIGH STREET c1955

Compare the High Street seen here to that of half a century ago. Road widening and the war contributed to the removal of the old buildings. The Vauxhall car speeding away down the road will not be seen today: only buses use the road during the day. The blank wall beyond the new work has been improved today by the addition of a huge mural.

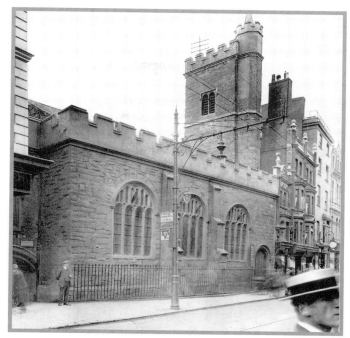

ST STEPHEN'S CHURCH 1924 76594

HIGH STREET c1955 E48073

HIGH STREET C1960 E48075

This shows the new work in more detail but not in any better light. These buildings surely deserve an award as a Site of Outstanding Natural Ugliness. In fairness, much of this was built soon after the war, when more suitable materials and skilled craftsmen were simply not available.

HIGH STREET C1965 E48096

This view looks along Sidwell Street to the junction of Paris Street. The concrete on the right is Debenhams. Beyond is Boots, still with the same clock today. But another building has now been fitted in between the two, still leaving room for North Street. A motor scooter turns right from Paris Street as a Ford Anglia van sets off on the right.

SIDWELL STREET c1965 E48094

With his camera further into Sidwell Street, still looking back towards the junction in photograph No E48096, our photographer captures this more modern scene. Sadly, he omitted to record the exact date of his trip: the Commer van indicates that it must have been 1968 or later, because the 'E' suffix on the registration mark was not introduced until January 1st that year. There is a remarkable lack of customers for the shops here.

HIGH STREET c1965 E48097

Here we see a rather bland redevelopment at the top of Paris Street, near its junction with the High Street. The road to the right is the entrance to the bus station - just the place you would expect to see a shop offering coach tours. The building is now an estate agent.

THE BUS AND COACH STATION C1965 E48090
The elegant coaches of this era are replaced today by dozens of small buses that buzz around this location, adding fuss (and a lot of exhaust smoke) to the rather languid scene captured here.

THE GUILDHALL 1896 38003
After the cathedral, this is probably the best (and oldest) building in town. It was originally 13th-century, and rebuilt a hundred years later. The portico overhanging the High Street was added during the reign of Queen Elizabeth I. The Turks Head Hotel next door is also ancient. Note the lady outside with a large basket: this was a small selling pitch for years.

THE GUILDHALL 1929 82292

Our photographer gained permission to climb to the second floor of the building opposite for this fine study of the Guildhall. As can be seen, the upper part has been renewed in more recent times. The balustrade is 18th-century.

HIGH STREET AND THE GUILDHALL 1929 82291
Mechanised transport is now plain to see. Sadly, the trams were already reaching the end of their working lives: just two years later, they were replaced by motor buses. Note the changes to the ground and first floors of the Turks Head compared to the earlier view. The trader's basket is still in evidence.

THE GUILDHALL c1955 E48006
By now, the traffic for which Exeter would become notorious is evident. The decorated iron standards that once carried both tram wires and street lighting are still in place. The clock above the jewellers H Samuel hangs there to this day.

THE GUILDHALL C1955 E48051

Although this view is supposed to have been taken around the same time as photograph No E48006, there are several significant changes between the two. Those elegant lamp standards have disappeared and have been replaced by modern concrete monstrosities.

THE GUILDHALL C1955 E48052

Our final view of the Guildhall examines the scene looking the opposite way, towards Fore Street. On the right, the building with a sun blind is still there, but the infill between it and the Guildhall has been replaced. Travel agents now occupy what was the Lotus shop. Today, the lamp posts have been removed and street lighting is fixed high on the walls of the buildings.

FORE STREET 1896 38007
This steep hill from the centre to the river was always a
busy place. The man on the extreme right appears to be
assembling the support pole for an awning. A feature of
dress a century ago was headwear. Every single person
in this view is wearing a hat, bonnet or cap.

FORE STREET 1896 38008
Another busy view of Fore Street. Note the man on
the extreme right working on the sign over the shop.
Our heath and safety police today would swoon at the
whole set-up. Copious quantities of horse manure can
be seen on the road surface.

ST MARY STEPS CHURCH 1912 64577
The Bone Mill to the right is no more, but the shabby building beyond has been returned to its Tudor glory by stripping off the surface rendering. The gable-ended building towards the left has been demolished; it was replaced by an older building that was carefully moved into place when road development threatened it. It is now known as 'The House that Moved'. The plaque on the wall to the left tells that the wall was part of the old West Gate.

STEPCOTE HILL 1911 63678

Instantly recognisable today, this road runs between St Mary Steps Church and the Tudor building seen in photograph No 64577. Only the dress of the passers-by has changed.

ON THE EXE 1896 38040

Here we see West Exeter from Mount Dinham. The railway (right) is the steep incline from Central station (London & South Western Railway) to St Davids (Great Western), where the smoke can be seen. The LSWR route to Plymouth via north Dartmoor had only been open 6 years when this photograph was taken.

EXE BRIDGE 1929 82300

Only the river remains of this view today; the rest is the victim of the onward march of the motor car. The elegant bridge was built in 1905 to accommodate trams - note the one that is crossing. It was replaced by two concrete monstrosities in the late 1960s, and now traffic screams around where the buildings once were. The city centre is to the right.

RIVER EXE AND THE BRIDGE 1929 82301
This view is a monument to a more relaxed age when a gentle row along the river Exe with wife or lady-friend was deemed pleasure enough. The trees growing alongside the river on the left are also consigned to history.

THE BRIDGE c1955 E48049
When this photograph was taken, the planners of the time would have been in the early stages of plotting the destruction of this scene. The Riverside Cafe and Hotel (now razed) was a popular spot, frequented by many who took their simple pleasures down by the river.

THE PORT 1896 38034

A little-known fact is that Exeter was the first place to be served by an artificial canal with locks. The Romans built several channels in the north, but this, constructed in 1566, pre-dated the northern canals where many people think the canal age started.

IN THE PORT 1896 38035

An indication of the kind of cargoes passing through the Port is gained from noting the wharfside businesses. W L Jones' bonded store (seen in No 38036) is now centre shot. The building (left) is a wholesale grocer and importers of sugar, fruit and Newfoundland fish. Many of these items would originate in the Americas.

IN THE PORT 1896 38036
Final improvements on the Exeter Canal, completed in 1832, allowed larger vessels, such as the 'Hans Emil'
pictured here, to reach the Port. Note the bonded warehouse to the left of centre.

IN THE PORT 1896 38037
The Exeter Canal was just over 5 miles long; trading
along it to these quays continued until 1972.
Subsequently, a maritime museum was established, but
this has now been dispersed, a victim of council
indifference. As the canal's owners, they seem
curiously at a loss to know how best to exploit this
wonderful asset.

THE CANAL 1929 82303

THE CANAL 1929
Less than a mile outside Exeter, the canal becomes delightfully rural. Swing bridges such as this are a feature of the navigation.

FROM THE CANAL 1929
At Trews Weir, water from the river Exe was diverted into the canal. The absence of trading vessels is made up for by the boy sitting on the quay, about to sail his model yacht.

FROM THE CANAL 1929 82302

FROM THE CANAL 1896 38033

Exactly what the lone oarsman is doing is open to speculation. Note the towing path to the left with a lady and child out for a stroll. Then, as now, this is a popular walk. The path extends for the full length of the canal.

VIEW FROM THE WEST 1896 38029

This view has gone for ever. Exwick Hill, where the cameraman stood over a century ago, is now covered with houses. A hay-rick can be seen in the field; the railway and river are a little further away. The spire of St Michael & All Angels is prominent to the left of the cathedral towers.

BRAMPFORD SPEKE, THE VILLAGE c1955 B385001

The cars are different now, and the houses are more brightly painted than their somewhat dull appearance in this view - but otherwise this portion of Bampford Speke is unchanged almost half a century later.

BRAMPFORD SPEKE, THE POST OFFICE c1955 B385002

It is almost inevitable, but the village post office is no more. The door is infilled and the place is now a house called Corner Cottage. For the visitor's delight, both buildings in this view retain their thatched roofs.

BROADCLYST
Killerton House from the Drive c1960
If this looks rather inviting, you are in luck. The mansion - dating from 1778 - is in the care of the National Trust, and is open to visitors. Built for the Acland family, the gardens have been extensively developed and are a delightful place to spend time.

◆

COUNTESS WEAR
The Village 1906
Countess Wear is a small village on the banks of the Exe, named after the 13th-century Countess of Devon, who caused a weir to be constructed here. It is an entirely unremarkable village; this view shows one of the prettier parts.

BROADCLYST, KILLERTON HOUSE FROM THE DRIVE c1960 B217020

COUNTESS WEAR, THE VILLAGE 1906 53980

COUNTESS WEAR, THE BRIDGE 1906 53981
Built in 1770, this bridge was (and is) the lowest crossing point on the river Exe (if you exclude the M5 motorway bridge, which is not a river crossing in the accepted sense). Note the fishermen with their nets. There used to be salmon in this river; today few are caught.

CREDITON

High Street 1896 37634

Two of the finer examples of the Victorian architect's skills are
to be seen here. Left is the Town Hall, which now houses the
tourist office and was never used by the council. Beneath the
roof, a somewhat pretentious inscription reads: 'Anno Decimo
Quinto Victoriae Reginae MDCCCLII'. To the right, the late
Victorian edifice is Lloyds Bank.

CREDITON, HIGH STREET 1904 52085
Gas is still the power source for street lighting in this view. The bank is now
the Nat West, whilst across the road Barnes' printers has acquired a rendered
front and a travel agent as tenant. Close to the group of people left of centre,
a striped barber's pole hangs over the pavement.

CREDITON, HIGH STREET AND THE SHIP HOTEL c1955 C183013

Fifty years after photograph No 52085, this view is little changed and still recognisable to this day. The poles carrying electric and telephone services have gone, as has the newsagent selling Gold Flake cigarettes. An insurance consultant now occupies this building. The cars dotted around evoke memories though: Standard Vanguard, MG, and Morris.

CREDITON, HIGH STREET c1955 C183012

After taking photograph No C183013, the photographer talked his way into the offices above the Nat West bank. Looking back along the High Street away from Exeter, we see the other end of the post-war cars.

CREDITON, HIGH STREET c1955 C183023
A view at the west end of the High Street. The pedestrian crossing with its Belisha beacons (named after the pre-war politician who introduced them) have disappeared today. Behind the wall to the right is Tanners Yard, an indication of the trade carried on there, together with a Congregational church.

CREDITON, HIGH STREET c1955 C183026
This view looks back towards the town centre from the west end. The scaffolded building on the left is High Street Chapel; the taxi company, together with the Shell petrol pump, do not exist today.

DUNSFORD, THE BRIDGE c1861 5817
This old bridge with segmented arches crosses the river Teign in the next valley west beyond Exeter. The whole area is part of the Dartmoor National Park. The bridge is known as Steps Bridge, and apart from the trees, the scene is unchanged after 140 years.

DUNSFORD, THE WEIR c1861 5818
This view was taken from the bridge. The woods to the right are now National Trust property and managed by the Devon Wildlife Trust. To the left is now the Steps Bridge Inn.

DUNSFORD, THE VILLAGE c1960 D118005

Dunsford is a long straggling village with several interesting features. In the timeless way of these rural backwaters, change does not come quickly. The house on the left (Orchard Cottage) still has the identical door in place.

DUNSFORD, THE VILLAGE c1960 D118007

The church of St Mary dominates the village. Its tower is 14th- and 15th-century, whilst the interior was rebuilt in 1846. On the road, a pub sign can be seen. This indicates the location of The Royal Oak.

DUNSFORD, THE VILLAGE c1960 D118015

We see thatch and cob a-plenty here. The rather run-down house on the left is now very smart, acting as a doctor's surgery. Cob was much used in this corner of England. A mix of straw and dried mud, it is completely reliable provided the thatched roof is kept waterproof and the base free from damp: stone is the preferred material for this.

DUNSFORD, BRITTON STREET c1960 D118018

A further example of this method of building. The dominant position of the church is clear from this photograph.

NEWTON ST CYRES, THE VILLAGE c1955 N83016

The main road from north Devon to Exeter is just a little busier today than when this view was taken. Indeed, it often needs great patience just to cross the road. This view is still to be seen, although the curving row of houses on the right have gone, replaced by a village green.

NEWTON ST CYRES, THE VILLAGE c1955 N83017

The village is unchanged today - another perfect example of the timelessness of this area. The buildings are better decorated, but the Shuttern Brook is still a ford.

NEWTON ST CYRES, THE VILLAGE c1955 N83018
Here the ford is viewed looking towards the main road. This view has changed dramatically today. The curved houses on the left beyond the ford have been demolished, all except the left and end one. Over the road (in the centre), nothing remains today.

NEWTON ST CYRES, THE PARISH CHURCH c1955 N83020
Unusually dedicated (to St Julitta and St Cyriac), Newton St Cyres parish church has seen several attempts at rebuilding over the centuries. Some of the tower is 13th-century, the rest 15th-century. It is attractive inside as well, worthy of a visit.

ROCKBEARE
The Village c1960

Rockbeare has suffered since this picture was taken by becoming a dormitory village for Exeter: a desirable place to live. Consequently, much of the old village is now surrounded by 'little boxes' loved by only those who own them. Scenes like this are now literally a thing of the past.

ROCKBEARE
The Church c1960

The church of St Mary in Rockbeare has little to commend it. One of those Victorian rebuilds that destroyed their character, St Mary's retains but a few fragments of what was before its 'treatment' in 1888. The lych gate (roughly where the photographer is standing) probably holds more interest.

ROCKBEARE, THE VILLAGE c1960 R257007

ROCKBEARE, THE CHURCH c1960 R257009

TEDBURN ST MARY, THE POST OFFICE c1955 T151004
There is still a post office in Tedburn St Mary: but not here. This is now subsumed into Rose Cottage alongside. The slate-roofed building beyond is a veterinary surgery.

TEDBURN ST MARY, THE KINGS ARMS c1955 T151006
The Kings Arms still serves fine food and a good selection of beers to wash it down. Opposite, the village stores still trades - albeit much modified. They do not sell National Benzole petrol as they did when this view was recorded.

TOPSHAM, THE STRAND 1906 53993

Views like this can still be seen in Topsham, for 20th-century building has been minimal. There is a strong Dutch influence in many of the houses, especially here on the Strand. Dutch trading ships carried bricks as ballast; these were used by the local merchants to build with, having Dutch architecture in mind.

TOPSHAM, THE QUAY 1906 53990
Topsham is a wonderful blend of old and new. Just look at these
characters idling on the quay, some of them really roguish-looking.
The Romans built a port here, and when Countess Wear blocked
navigation to Exeter, it became the prime port for this area. Today, it is
given over to leisure boating, although there is a ferry across the river
towards extensive walks and the canal.

WOODBURY, THE VILLAGE 1906 53995

At least the road in Woodbury is now surfaced. Here, it appears to be in a dreadful state. The post office (centre) is an antique shop today, whilst the building to the right is The Maltsters Arms. Another pub, The White Horse, is along the street to the left.

WOODBURY, THE VILLAGE c1955 W129006

Looking more or less the opposite way from photograph No 53995, our photographer catches the essential peace of this village. The house on the left is still not a pub, and the telephone kiosk has not moved. The war memorial has. It was in the way of a road improvement scheme and has been re-sited on the green a few yards behind the camera.

WOODBURY, THE PARISH CHURCH 1906 53996

St Swithin's is another church inexpertly restored in the 19th century. The small stream that makes the ford is now piped underground, and today's children do not need a rickety plank to keep their feet dry.

WOODBURY, THE VILLAGE c1955 W129009

At the top end of the village, half a century on, the pleasant thatched building has gone, replaced by a modern house set back from the road. Next door are the Church Rooms. The shop (left) is no more, but the village pump is still in place.

WOODBURY, THE VILLAGE c1955 W129002

The main road between Exeter and Budleigh Salterton runs through Woodbury. This tranquil scene is replaced by constant traffic. The creeper on the house is no more, neither is the left hand pole. The scene is recorded as taken circa 1955. . . .

WOODBURY, THE VILLAGE c1955 W129020

. . . as is this one, a few yards further down the road. But the road has been improved between our photographer's visits. The carriageway has been resurfaced and white lines added. The exact date of this view must be open to question, however, as the car in view is a Mini: they were not introduced until August 1959.

Index

Frith Book Co Titles

Frith Book Company publish over a 100 new titles each year. For latest catalogue please contact Frith Book Co.

Town Books 96pp, 100 photos. County and Themed Books 128pp, 150 photos
(unless specified) All titles hardback laminated case and jacket
except those indicated pb (paperback)

Around Barnstaple	1-85937-084-5	£12.99
Around Blackpool	1-85937-049-7	£12.99
Around Bognor Regis	1-85937-055-1	£12.99
Around Bristol	1-85937-050-0	£12.99
Around Cambridge	1-85937-092-6	£12.99
Cheshire	1-85937-045-4	£14.99
Around Chester	1-85937-090-X	£12.99
Around Chesterfield	1-85937-071-3	£12.99
Around Chichester	1-85937-089-6	£12.99
Cornwall	1-85937-054-3	£14.99
Cotswolds	1-85937-099-3	£14.99
Around Derby	1-85937-046-2	£12.99
Devon	1-85937-052-7	£14.99
Dorset	1-85937-075-6	£14.99
Dorset Coast	1-85937-062-4	£14.99
Around Dublin	1-85937-058-6	£12.99
East Anglia	1-85937-059-4	£14.99
Around Eastbourne	1-85937-061-6	£12.99
English Castles	1-85937-078-0	£14.99
Around Falmouth	1-85937-066-7	£12.99
Hampshire	1-85937-064-0	£14.99
Isle of Man	1-85937-065-9	£14.99
Around Maidstone	1-85937-056-X	£12.99
North Yorkshire	1-85937-048-9	£14.99
Around Nottingham	1-85937-060-8	£12.99
Around Penzance	1-85937-069-1	£12.99
Around Reading	1-85937-087-X	£12.99
Around St Ives	1-85937-068-3	£12.99
Around Salisbury	1-85937-091-8	£12.99
Around Scarborough	1-85937-104-3	£12.99
Scottish Castles	1-85937-077-2	£14.99
Around Sevenoaks and Tonbridge	1-85937-057-8	£12.99

Sheffield and S Yorkshire	1-85937-070-5	£14.99
Shropshire	1-85937-083-7	£14.99
Staffordshire	1-85937-047-0 (96pp)	£12.99
Suffolk	1-85937-074-8	£14.99
Surrey	1-85937-081-0	£14.99
Around Torbay	1-85937-063-2	£12.99
Wiltshire	1-85937-053-5	£14.99
Around Bakewell	1-85937-113-2	£12.99
Around Bournemouth	1-85937-067-5	£12.99
Cambridgeshire	1-85937-086-1	£14.99
Essex	1-85937-082-9	£14.99
Around Great Yarmouth	1-85937-085-3	£12.99
Hertfordshire	1-85937-079-9	£14.99
Isle of Wight	1-85937-114-0	£14.99
Around Lincoln	1-85937-111-6	£12.99
Oxfordshire	1-85937-076-4	£14.99
Around Shrewsbury	1-85937-110-8	£12.99
South Devon Coast	1-85937-107-8	£14.99
Around Stratford upon Avon	1-85937-098-5	£12.99
West Midlands	1-85937-109-4	£14.99

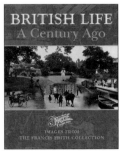

British Life A Century Ago
246 x 189mm
144pp, hardback.
Black and white
Lavishly illustrated with photos from the turn of the century, and with extensive commentary. It offers a unique insight into the social history and heritage of bygone Britain.

1-85937-103-5 £17.99

Available from your local bookshop or from the publisher

Frith Book Co Titles Available in 2000

Around Bath	1-85937-097-7	£12.99	Mar
County Durham	1-85937-123-x	£14.99	Mar
Cumbria	1-85937-101-9	£14.99	Mar
Down the Thames	1-85937-121-3	£14.99	Mar
Around Exeter	1-85937-126-4	£12.99	Mar
Greater Manchester	1-85937-108-6	£14.99	Mar
Around Guildford	1-85937-117-5	£12.99	Mar
Around Harrogate	1-85937-112-4	£12.99	Mar
Around Leicester	1-85937-073-x	£12.99	Mar
Around Liverpool	1-85937-051-9	£12.99	Mar
Around Newark	1-85937-105-1	£12.99	Mar
Northumberland and Tyne & Wear			
	1-85937-072-1	£14.99	Mar
Around Oxford	1-85937-096-9	£12.99	Mar
Around Plymouth	1-85937-119-1	£12.99	Mar
Around Southport	1-85937-106-x	£12.99	Mar
Welsh Castles	1-85937-120-5	£14.99	Mar
Around Belfast	1-85937-094-2	£12.99	Apr
Canals and Waterways	1-85937-129-9	£17.99	Apr
Down the Severn	1-85937-118-3	£14.99	Apr
East Sussex	1-85937-130-2	£14.99	Apr
Exmoor	1-85937-132-9	£14.99	Apr
Gloucestershire	1-85937-102-7	£14.99	Apr
Around Horsham	1-85937-127-2	£12.99	Apr
Around Ipswich	1-85937-133-7	£12.99	Apr
Ireland (pb)	1-85937-181-7	£9.99	Apr
Kent Living Memories	1-85937-125-6	£14.99	Apr
London (pb)	1-85937-183-3	£9.99	Apr
New Forest	1-85937-128-0	£14.99	Apr
Scotland (pb)	1-85937-182-5	£9.99	Apr
Around Southampton	1-85937-088-8	£12.99	Apr
Stone Circles & Ancient Monuments			
	1-85937-143-4	£17.99	Apr
Sussex (pb)	1-85937-184-1	£9.99	Apr
Colchester (pb)	1-85937-188-4	£8.99	May
County Maps of Britain			
	1-85937-156-6 (192pp)	£19.99	May
Leicestershire (pb)	1-85937-185-x	£9.99	May

Lincolnshire	1-85937-135-3	£14.99	May
Around Newquay	1-85937-140-x	£12.99	May
Nottinghamshire (pb)	1-85937-187-6	£9.99	May
Redhill to Reigate	1-85937-137-x	£12.99	May
Victorian & Edwardian Yorkshire			
	1-85937-154-x	£14.99	May
Around Winchester	1-85937-139-6	£12.99	May
Yorkshire (pb)	1-85937-186-8	£9.99	May
Berkshire (pb)	1-85937-191-4	£9.99	Jun
Brighton (pb)	1-85937-192-2	£8.99	Jun
Dartmoor	1-85937-145-0	£14.99	Jun
East London	1-85937-080-2	£14.99	Jun
Glasgow (pb)	1-85937-190-6	£8.99	Jun
Kent (pb)	1-85937-189-2	£9.99	Jun
Victorian & Edwardian Kent			
	1-85937-149-3	£14.99	Jun
North Devon Coast	1-85937-146-9	£14.99	Jun
Peak District	1-85937-100-0	£14.99	Jun
Around Truro	1-85937-147-7	£12.99	Jun
Victorian & Edwardian Maritime Album			
	1-85937-144-2	£17.99	Jun
West Sussex	1-85937-148-5	£14.99	Jun
Churches of Berkshire	1-85937-170-1	£17.99	Jul
Churches of Dorset	1-85937-172-8	£17.99	Jul
Churches of Hampshire	1-85937-207-4	£17.99	Jul
Churches of Wiltshire	1-85937-171-x	£17.99	Jul
Derbyshire (pb)	1-85937-196-5	£9.99	Jul
Edinburgh (pb)	1-85937-193-0	£8.99	Jul
Herefordshire	1-85937-174-4	£14.99	Jul
Norwich (pb)	1-85937-194-9	£8.99	Jul
Ports and Harbours	1-85937-208-2	£17.99	Jul
Somerset and Avon	1-85937-153-1	£14.99	Jul
South Devon Living Memories			
	1-85937-168-x	£14.99	Jul
Warwickshire (pb)	1-85937-203-1	£9.99	Jul
Worcestershire	1-85937-152-3	£14.99	Jul
Yorkshire Living Memories			
	1-85937-166-3	£14.99	Jul

FRITH PRODUCTS & SERVICES

Francis Frith would doubtless be pleased to know that the pioneering publishing venture he started in 1860 still continues today. More than a hundred and thirty years later, The Francis Frith Collection continues in the same innovative tradition and is now one of the foremost publishers of vintage photographs in the world. Some of the current activities include:

Interior Decoration

Today Frith's photographs can be seen framed and as giant wall murals in thousands of pubs, restaurants, hotels, banks, retail stores and other public buildings throughout the country. In every case they enhance the unique local atmosphere of the places they depict and provide reminders of gentler days in an increasingly busy and frenetic world.

Product Promotions

Frith products have been used by many major companies to promote the sales of their own products or to reinforce their own history and heritage. Brands include Hovis bread, Courage beers, Scots Porage Oats, Colman's mustard, Cadbury's foods, Mellow Birds coffee, Dunhill pipe tobacco, Guinness, and Bulmer's Cider.

Genealogy and Family History

As the interest in family history and roots grows world-wide, more and more people are turning to Frith's photographs of Great Britain for images of the towns, villages and streets where their ancestors lived; and, of course, photographs of the churches and chapels where their ancestors were christened, married and buried are an essential part of every genealogy tree and family album.

A series of easy-to-use CD Roms is planned for publication, and an increasing number of Frith photographs will be able to be viewed on specialist genealogy sites. A growing range of Frith books will be available on CD.

The Internet

Already thousands of Frith photographs can be viewed and purchased on the internet. By the end of the year 2000 some 60,000 Frith photographs will be available on the internet. The number of sites is constantly expanding, each focussing on different products and services from the Collection.

Some of the sites are listed below.

www.townpages.co.uk
www.icollector.com
www.barclaysquare.co.uk
www.cornwall-online.co.uk

For background information on the Collection look at the three following sites:

www.francisfrith.com
www.francisfrith.co.uk
www.frithbook.co.uk

Frith Products

All Frith photographs are available Framed or just as Mounted Prints, and can be ordered from the address below. From time to time other products - Address Books, Calendars, Table Mats, etc - are available.

For further information:
if you would like further information on any of the above aspects of the Frith business please contact us at the address below:
The Francis Frith Collection,
Frith's Barn, Teffont, Salisbury, Wiltshire,
England SP3 5QP.
Tel: +44 (0)1722 716 376 Fax: +44 (0)1722 716 881   Email: uksales@francisfrith.com

---

To receive your FREE Mounted Print

Cut out this Voucher and return it with your remittance for £1.50 to cover postage and handling. Choose any photograph included in this book. Your SEPIA print will be A4 in size, and mounted in a cream mount with burgundy rule lines, overall size 14 x 11 inches.

Order additional Mounted Prints at HALF PRICE (only £7.49 each*)

If there are further pictures you would like to order, possibly as gifts for friends and family, acquire them at half price (no additional postage and handling required).

Have your Mounted Prints framed*

For an additional £14.95 per print you can have your chosen Mounted Print framed in an elegant polished wood and gilt moulding, overall size 16 x 13 inches (no additional postage and handling required).

---

* IMPORTANT!
These special prices are only available if ordered using the original voucher on this page (no copies permitted) and at the same time as your free Mounted Print, for delivery to the same address

---

Frith Collectors' Guild

From time to time we publish a magazine of news and stories about Frith photographs and further special offers of Frith products. If you would like 12 months FREE membership, please return this form.

Send completed forms to:
The Francis Frith Collection, Frith's Barn, Teffont, Salisbury, Wiltshire SP3 5QP

Voucher for FREE and Reduced Price Frith Prints

Picture no.	Page number	Qty	Mounted @ £7.49	Framed + £14.95	Total Cost
		1	**Free of charge***	£	£
			£7.49	£	£
			£7.49	£	£
			£7.49	£	£
			£7.49	£	£
			£7.49	£	£
			* Post & handling		£1.50
Book Title			**Total Order Cost**		£

Please do not photocopy this voucher. Only the original is valid, so please cut it out and return it to us.

I enclose a cheque / postal order for £ . . . . made payable to 'The Francis Frith Collection'
OR please debit my Mastercard / Visa / Switch / Amex card

Number . . . .

Expires . . . .   Signature . . . .

Name Mr/Mrs/Ms . . . .

Address . . . .

. . . .

. . . .

. . . .

. . . . Postcode . . . .

Daytime Tel No . . . .   Valid to 31/12/01

The Francis Frith Collectors' Guild

Please enrol me as a member for 12 months free of charge.

Name Mr/Mrs/Ms . . . .

Address . . . .

. . . .

. . . . Postcode . . . .

Free Print - see overleaf